Southbou

Advice
to Northerners Moving
South

written by Heath and Susan Coleman

art by Michael ClenDening

DOBERDOR PUBLISHING

Library of Congress Cataloging in Publication Data

Coleman, Heath C., living
Coleman, Susan H., living also
Southbound: Advice to Northerners Moving South

Library of Congress Catalog Card Number: 96-96414

ISBN 0-9652350-0-9

Introduction

I led a sheltered youth to say the least with respect to the differences both actual and supposed, fostered in people by geographical separation. It was not until after my college graduation and the commencement of my career in a job that required me to speak daily to people in or from the north that I was exposed to both the cultural diversity and the lack there of.

The majority of the people I worked with over the years were transplanted from the north. **Some adapted very well. Some did not.**

Regardless of where you are from, if you are reading this collection of my observations to be amused, I hope you will be. If you are in fact about to, or already have, relocated south you may just find parts of this useful.

Heath Coleman

Introduction, too

I was raised in the north by parents who were raised in the north. Luckily, I moved to Nashville, Tennessee in 1980 and have lived south of the Mason-Dixon ever since. While I enjoy visiting "up there" I have no desire to live in a place where you need to shovel the driveway so you can go to work. In the South, if you need to shovel the driveway there is too much snow on the roads to get to work.

I now find myself married to a life long Southerner and some pretty humorous misunderstandings have resulted from this cross cultural union. For instance, Southerners refer to stocking caps as "toboggans". Since I grew up riding toboggans (a sled-like device) in the snow, the thought of people wearing toboggans on their heads in hope of keeping warm, is extremely amusing to me. As I tried to explain this reaction to Heath, he gazed at me not comprehending and insisted, "That is not funny!".

Between his "southern mumbling", and my Yankee idioms and assumptions, we have to sort things out pretty regularly, but somehow it works.

I hope you enjoy this collection of thoughts and observations as much as we enjoyed putting it together.

Susan Coleman

For Gary

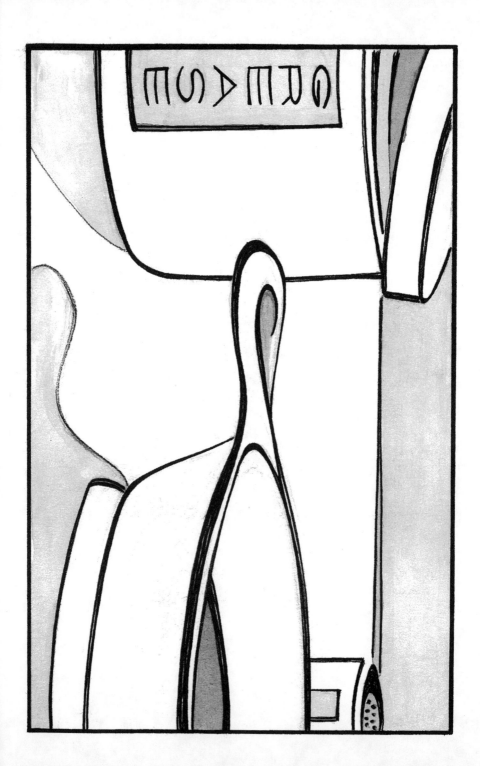

Save all manner of bacon grease. You will be instructed later how to use it.

Purchase and wear a pinky ring. This will make Southerners trust you immediately.

Tell this joke as often as possible:

Q: What does a Southerner call a Northerner?

A: Boss.

Southerners love this joke. It is particularly effective if you are the boss.

All Southerners are honest.

If a **Southerner** does harass, con, abuse or rob you, he will at least smile and be polite while doing it.

Crawdaddy is another name for gulf shrimp.

If you are invited snipe hunting, accept immediately.

Bush hogging has nothing to do with hunting wild pigs.

If you forget a **Southerner's** name, refer to him (or her) as "Bubba". You have a **75%** chance of being right.

If someone in your family is named Guido, mention him (or her) often.

Change your own name to Guido.

Just because you can drive on snow and ice, does not mean we can . **Stay home the two** days of the year it snows.

If you do run your car into a ditch, don't panic. Four men in the cab of a four wheel drive with a 12-pack of beer and a tow chain will be along shortly. Don't try to help them. Just stay out of their way. This is what they live for.

Don't be surprised to find movie rentals and bait in the same store.

Do not buy food at the movie store.

If, when visiting a *Southerner's* home for dinner, his wife asks him to clear the table and he does so with a shotgun, do not be alarmed. Politely excuse yourself and leave, for there is about to be a domestic quarrel.

If you shout to your southern neighbor, "Come look at the snake!", he will arrive with a shotgun, hoe, shovel and pickax. Then, like a golf caddy, he will pick the proper weapon dependent on the size and make of the snake. This is a deeply ingrained biblical thing in all southern men. Even if you meant for him to just look at the snake, do not interfere.

You no longer have to make three right turns to go left. Unless you want to.

If it can't be fried in bacon grease, it ain't worth cooking, let alone eating.

When visiting a new southern friend's home for the first time, comment on his belongings in this order:

1. Dog
2. Bass boat
3. Firebird up on blocks in the yard
4. Any visible fire arms
5. Quality of the blocks holding up the trailer

If asked to go deer hunting with a group of Southerners, go, but do not bother to take a gun.

The Bible Belt is <u>not</u> a garment worn to church.

Remember:

"Y'all" is singular.

"All y'all" is plural.

"All y'all's" is plural possessive.

There is nothing sillier than a Northerner imitating a southern accent, unless it is a Southerner imitating a Boston accent.

Get used to hearing, "You ain't from around here are you?"

In some cases you may want to say, "Yes, I am from here. I just have a cold."

In some cases you should say nothing.

When you visit back north, your friends and family will remark that you have changed. This is not necessarily a bad thing.

This may be where your children will say they are from.

People walk slower here.

Upon my first call to serve for jury duty in a small Alabama town, the judge asked if any of the 100 or so prospective jurors were related to the defendant. This literally cleared half the courtroom.

"Fixin' to", has nothing to do with repair, reconstruction, or halting the natural reproduction of animals. It means, "about to do".

When meeting new southern friends, be sure to mention how nice it is to have been transferred to the South where the cost of living is low and you still retain your northern salary. They will be pleased to know you are doing so well.

Don't be worried that you don't understand anyone. They don't understand you either.

The first southern expression to creep into a transplanted Northerner's vocabulary is the adjective "big ol'", as in "big ol' truck" or "big ol' boy". Eighty-five percent begin their new southern influenced dialect with this expression. One hundred percent are in denial about it.

Some Northerners gain a fine grasp of the southern dialect but very few ever learn to speak or understand the next phase, "southern mumbling".

The proper pronunciation you learned in school is no longer proper.

To speak proper Southern you must shorten all multi-syllable words into as few syllables as possible.

To speak proper Southern you must stretch all single syllable words into more syllables than you thought possible.

During a meeting at work, the secretary mentioned the "year end banquet". I noticed the look of puzzlement and concern on the face of an employee who had only been there a few days. What he thought he heard the secretary say (with a southern accent), was "urine banquet". He had just returned from the drug test given to all new employees, and thought we were very serious about this urine thing.

"Whad'ya' lack?", may mean, "how much do you have to go?", or, "What do you prefer?".
You must consider the context of the question.

"Does a chicken have lips?", means no.

"Better than pockets on a shirt.", is good.

"Better than handles on a suitcase.", is real good.

"Does a bear shit in the woods?", is an assured, "Yes!"

When a new southern friend introduces you to his wife, be sure to ask if she is a cousin from his mother's or father's side. He will appreciate your interest in his family lineage.

To fit in, you will need to make some addition to your name such as, Billy Joe, Billy Bud, Billy Bob, or Billy Ray. As you can see, you will need to change your first name to Billy. Franky Joe or Sally Bud just doesn't sound right.

Be Advised:

The "He needed killin'" defense is valid here.

If a *Southerner* offers to carry you, he will not try to physically pick you up. He is only offering you a ride in his car.

Had he actually been willing to tote you, he would have said so.

When a new southern friend invites you to attend his church, go at least once.

If attending a funeral in the *South*, remember, we stay until the last shovel of dirt is thrown on and the tent is torn down.

If you are invited to a southern bridal shower go ahead and purchase the baby gift. They will need it in six to seven months.

Honoring the king is an important part of southern living. Before inviting new southern friends over, purchase and display the finest velvet Elvis money can buy.

Be warned: If you order dark toast in the south, it will be white bread burnt to a crisp. If you want wheat toast, say wheat toast.

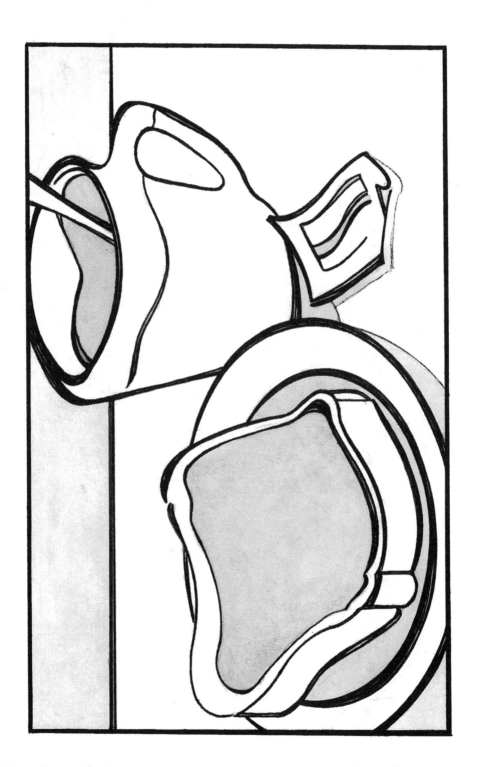

At this point, in this literary endeavor, the letters "GD" and "F" shall stand for curse words. If you don't understand what these abbreviations stand for, you won't have to ask many friends before you get the right answer.

While there are people who find any foul language offensive, the general rule is that Southerners are much more offended by "GD" than "F" while the reverse seems to be true for Northerners.

You will notice the land value is lower. How much the land is valued is not necessarily as low.

Be sure that each time you are in a social setting with new southern friends, you make reference to southern inbreeding. You will be the life of the party.

If you are double-dog dared to do something, you must.

If you hear a Southerner exclaim, "Hey, y'all, watch this!" stay out of his way. These are likely the last words he will ever say.

Most Southerners do not use turn signals, and they ignore those who do. In fact, if you see a signal blinking on a car with a southern license plate, you may rest assured that it was on when the car was purchased.

Northerners can be identified by the spit on the inside of their car's windshield that comes from yelling at other drivers.

Just why are you in such a hurry?

On September 1st when you remark, "Thank God! It's finally time for it to cool off!", your new southern friends aren't laughing at you. They're laughing _near_ you.

That winter wardrobe you always brought out
in September can wait until November.

When moving into your new southern home, have the moving men leave the freezer on the front porch. This way you won't look out of place.

"I don't care to," in Southern means, "I don't mind," which makes sense if you think about it.*

* There is a dissenting opinion on this--S.C.

If you marry a Southerner, be prepared for the fact that you won't always understand each other. Of course, if you marry anyone you won't anyway, so what's the difference?

If there is the prediction of the slightest chance of even the most minuscule accumulation of snow, your presence is required at the local grocery store. It does not matter if you need anything from the store, it is just something you're supposed to do.

You will find that many Southerners have a deafness that comes and goes. To announce that the deafness has once again passed and that their auditory nerve has returned to full effectiveness, they will from time to time exclaim, "I heard that!"

A discussion of the weather between Southerners will sound like this:

First Southerner: "It's fixin' to snow!"

Second Southerner: "We better git to the store!"

First Southerner: "I heard that!"

Satellite dishes are very popular in the South. When you purchase one it is to be positioned directly in front of your trailer. This is logical bearing in mind that the dish cost considerably more than the trailer and should, therefore, be displayed.

East Texas Burglar Alarm: The "chick-chuck" of a 12 gauge pump. This is one of the few burglar alarms that is more alarming to the burglar than the resident.

If a Southerner says that you must have fallen off the back of the turnip truck, he is referring to your obvious good health and sensible diet including all of the important vegetables.

An integral part of southern living is going visiting. As a child I remember that as we were leaving, the host would often say, "ya'll stay with us". We never did. Perhaps it would be interesting if you tried staying to see what would happen.

For a man to be a true **Southerner**, it is necessary for him to quit his job and stay home, insuring that all beer breweries have a stable market. It is, of course, necessary for his wife to have a job so this southern tradition can be carried out. Whether you explain this to her before you move to the **South**, or after, is up to you.

Have you noticed that the only difference between the southern redneck and the northern redneck is the accent?

A popular topic of conversation among southern men is the number of divorces that they have gone through. This topic is fit in somewhere between their display and explanation of any body scars, and the grossest thing they did that day.

I am sure some Northern states are the same, but in the South a man can pronounce alimony as, "all the money". If you have carried out the tip on page 72 correctly, this should not be a problem.

Misunderstandings between Southerners and Northerners are completely possible without either of you being an idiot. If you marry one, from time to time you will be an idiot. Of course that isn't caused by where you are from. Is it?

Tornadoes and *Southerners* going through a divorce have a lot in common. In either case, you know someone is going to lose a trailer.

The proper pronunciation is neckid. Remember this if you propose marriage to a Southerner.

Neckid is usually an adjective. Used as a verb, it is "get neckid".

Florida is not considered a southern state. There are far more Yankees than Southerners living there.

Little country stores on two lane highways can be wondrous places. If you are impatient and in a hurry you won't enjoy them.

If you offer a Southerner a pop, he might pop you, just to get the first lick in.

In southern churches you will hear the hymn, All Glory, Laud and Honor. You will also hear expressions such as, "Laud, have mercy", "Good Laud", and "Laudy, Laudy, Laudy".

As you are cursing the person driving 15 m.p.h. in a 55 m.p.h. zone, directly in the middle of the road, remember, many folks learned to drive on a model of vehicle known as John Deere, and this is the proper speed and lane position for that vehicle.

You can ask a Southerner for directions, but unless you already know the positions of key hills, trees and rocks, you're better off to try to find it yourself.

When you move, arrange for a subscription to your hometown paper to be sent to your new southern address.

A friend from Chicago once read me the headline from that morning's paper. It said, "Highs in the seventies, eleven dead". He explained to me that as soon as the weather starts to get nice, the murder rate increases. I don't know if this is a broad northern occurrence or is isolated to Chicago, but I don't believe the spring season has this effect on any southern cities that I know of.

When you receive your new southern driver's license, you will also be issued a chain to hook your keys to your belt, a belt buckle with your name on it, and a baseball cap from the feed store of your choice.

Your new southern friends will inform you how lucky you are to be residing in their state rather than one of the less desirable neighboring states.

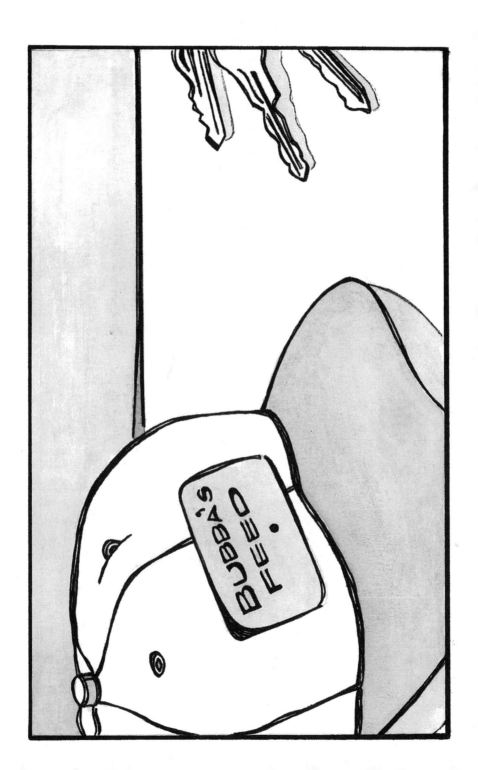

Pillar: Found in southern homes, used to prop things up.

A cotton or goose down pillar is ideal for propping oneself up in bed on **S**unday morning to watch bass fishing on the TV.

Porch pillars are to make the rocking chair more comfortable.

The roof is propped up with **2** by **4**'s.

There was an old man sitting on the road between two cities. A traveler stopped and asked the old man what the city ahead was like. The old man asked what the city he came from was like. The traveler said it was awful, depressing and backward. The old man said, "So is the city ahead". A second traveler stopped and asked, "How is the city ahead?". The man asked what the city he came from was like. The traveler said it was wonderful, bright and cheerful. The old man said, "So is the city ahead".

I have known transplanted Northerners who *will* always be Northerners. Some were happy, some were not. I have known Northerners who immediately became *Southerners regardless* of accent or other peripheral things. All of these people were happy. What and who you are is a state of mind, not of geography.

Some transplanted Northerners move here with their jobs and count the days until they can retire and go home. It seems a terrible thing, having to wait for happiness.

The biggest waste is to spend your time hating, whether it is a place, a person, or another way of life.

This book of rules is valid anywhere in the South except Texas. They have their own.

If you wish to order Southbound: Advice to Northerners Moving South, please send $6.95 per book (check or money order) to:

Doberdor Publishing, Inc.
Box 490-A
Lacey's Spring, AL 35754

Shipping is $1.75 for 1 book, $1.25 for each additional book. Alabama residents, please add 8% sales tax.